TEL AVIV
THE CITY AT A GLANCE

Tayelet
Tel Aviv's Mediterranean promenade, with its
string of beaches, is its year-round playground.
See p086

Kerem Hateimanim
The city's Yemenite quarter, lo
Carmel Market, boasts great N
eateries. Many of its dilapidat
been snapped up by savvy inv

GW00703484

Nahalat Binyamin
A pedestrian mall lined with I
and retro-cool hummus parlo
ranging from art nouveau to

Tel Aviv Port
Built in the 1930s, Tel Aviv's main port has
been transformed in recent years, and now
boasts high-end restaurants and boutiques.
See p014

Dizengoff Center
Set on the buzzy boulevard named after the
city's first mayor, Meir Dizengoff, this 1970s mall
is the heart of the main shopping district.
See p010

Yoo Towers
Philippe Starck's twin towers were the city's
first starchitect-designed residential project.
Mordechai Namir Road

Kirya
Identified by its communications tower,
this is Tel Aviv's city-centre military HQ.
Shaul Hamelech Boulevard

Azrieli Center
This three-building complex is a major city
landmark as well as a commercial hub.
See p064

INTRODUCTION
THE CHANGING FACE OF THE URBAN SCENE

Enviable urban assets are probably the last things most travellers envisage when they think of Tel Aviv – Israel's secular, seafront, commercial and cultural capital. But the world's first modern Jewish city is well and truly blessed with many of the amenities needed to be a sophisticated global destination. Ringed by 13km of beaches, lined with eye-catching locals with year-round tans and perpetual smiles, Tel Aviv is aggressively permissive, tolerant and open-minded – a blend of European progressiveness spiced with Levantine and Arab traditions. Like the rest of Israel, the city is slowly receding from headlines about war and terror. Instead the buzz is about its culinary scene, contemporary art fairs, designers and its growing amount of world-class architecture. The World Heritage Site of White City, and its trove of almost 5,000 Bauhaus buildings, is the city's most important offering, but aficionados are also now paying attention to Tel Aviv's Levantine, Ottoman-era and eclectic architecture.

True, this city must still deal with ongoing conflict both in and around Israel. Yet, more than a century after it rose from the sand, Tel Aviv retains much of the vision and the vigour of its original settlers. Resolutely Jewish, but today as gay, multicultural and wealthy as many European cities, it remains a place in a hurry. For the increasing number of tourists arriving here, there are ample reasons to slow down and enjoy the ride.

ESSENTIAL INFO

FACTS, FIGURES AND USEFUL ADDRESSES

TOURIST OFFICE
Information Bureau
46 Herbert Samuel Street
T 516 6188
www.visit-tlv.com

TRANSPORT
Car hire
Avis
T 529 9607
Hertz
T 975 4505
Egged Buses
T 694 8888
Israel Railway
T 577 4000
Taxis
Acropolis Taxis
T 561 9988

EMERGENCY SERVICES
Ambulance
T 101
Fire
T 102
Police
T 100
24-hour pharmacy
Superpharm
London Ministore Mall
Shaul Hamelech Boulevard
T 696 0106

EMBASSIES
British Embassy
192 Hayarkon Street
T 725 1222
www.britemb.org.il
US Embassy
71 Hayarkon Street
T 519 7575
telaviv.usembassy.gov

MONEY
American Express
32 Ben Yehuda Street
T 526 8888

POSTAL SERVICES
Post office
29 Hamered Street
T 510 3735
Shipping
UPS
T 577 0100
www.ups.com

BOOKS
A Place in History: Modernism, Tel Aviv, and the Creation of Jewish Urban Space
by Barbara Mann (Stanford University Press)
Revival of the Bauhaus in Tel Aviv
by Shmuel Yavin (BT Batsford)

WEBSITES
Architecture
www.artlog.co.il/telaviv
Art/Design
www.tamuseum.com
Newspapers
www.haaretz.com
www.jpost.com

COST OF LIVING
Taxi from Ben-Gurion Airport to city centre
143 shekels
Cappuccino
19 shekels
Packet of cigarettes
24 shekels
Daily newspaper
6 shekels
Bottle of champagne
390 shekels

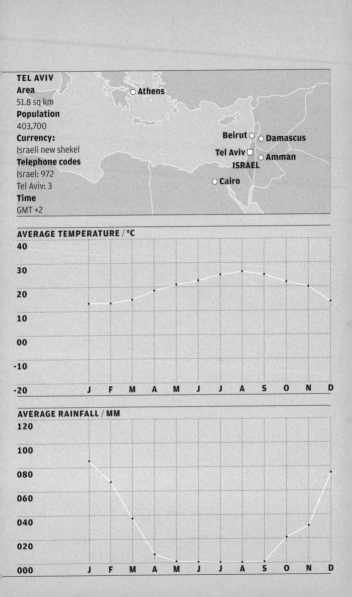

TEL AVIV
Area
51.8 sq km
Population
403,700
Currency:
Israeli new shekel
Telephone codes
Israel: 972
Tel Aviv: 3
Time
GMT +2

Athens

Beirut Damascus
Tel Aviv Amman
ISRAEL
Cairo

AVERAGE TEMPERATURE / °C

40											
30											
20											
10											
00											
-10											
-20| J	F	M	A	M	J	J	A	S	O	N	D

AVERAGE RAINFALL / MM

120											
100											
080											
060											
040											
020											
000| J	F	M	A	M	J	J	A	S	O	N	D

NEIGHBOURHOODS

THE AREAS YOU NEED TO KNOW AND WHY

To help you navigate the city, we've chosen the most interesting districts (see the map inside the back cover) and underlined featured venues in colour, according to their location (see below); those venues that are outside these areas are not coloured.

OLD JAFFA

One of the world's oldest cities, Jaffa is a compelling mix of east and west. Visit its fleamarket (Yefet Street), Historic District and the Ilana Goor Museum (4 Mazel Dagim Street, T 683 7676), home of the Israeli sculptor and furniture maker. Have lunch at The Container (see p047).

NOGA AND NEVEH TZEDEK

Straddling the border between Tel Aviv and Jaffa, Noga is the city's creative hub, peppered with galleries and media firms. The 'Oasis of Justice', or Neveh Tzedek (see p028), was Tel Aviv's first Jewish quarter, founded in 1887 by Aharon Shlush. After decades of neglect, shrewd investors are snapping up its airy Ottoman-era homes.

SHEINKIN

For Tel Avivians, Sheinkin is more of a way of life than a mere street. Named after the early Zionist activist Menahem Sheinkin, famed for giving his adopted city the name Tel Aviv, or Hill of Spring, it's lined with restaurants and chic boutiques (see p072). It's particularly buzzy on the Sabbath.

TAYELET

Officially called Herbert Samuel Hayarkon, this 6km seafront promenade, dubbed the Tayelet (see p086), defines the city's western boundary. Its wide stone walkway, dotted with pergolas, palm trees and snack kiosks, attracts joggers, dog-walkers and strollers. Think Miami on the Med.

GAN HAHASHMAL

Hebrew for Electric Garden, this area was the home of Israel's first power station in 1923. It was also the city's red-light district until the 1990s, when regeneration lured young Tel Avivians, and a nascent local fashion scene found an affordable home. Interesting shops and eateries now reign.

DIZENGOFF

The city's main retail corridor, Dizengoff has had a sartorial renaissance in recent years. A crop of independent boutiques (see p072) now rubs shoulders with the flagships of Israel's mega-brands in the Dizengoff Center (see p010). Architecture buffs should make a beeline for the Bauhaus Center (99 Dizengoff Street, T 522 0249).

WHITE CITY

This unique area boasts the world's richest concentration of Bauhaus buildings, with the majority dating from the early 1930s to the 1950s, and includes designs by Dov Carmi and Josef Neufeld. There are several good eateries here too, such as Social Club (see p036) and Tzfon Abraxas (see p046).

TEL AVIV PORT

Architect Tzadik Elyakim's flair and a multimillion-dollar makeover resurrected the port (see p014) in 2002. Its promenade now sports upmarket restaurants and nightlife. Free jazz performances and the antiques and organic food markets here are other highlights of the area.

LANDMARKS

THE SHAPE OF THE CITY SKYLINE

Blame it on Tel Aviv's youth – it's barely 100 years old – and rather flat, lifeless topography, but this city has relatively few major landmarks. There's no Western Wall or Dome of the Rock, as in Jerusalem, or anything like the Bahá'i Gardens, located high on a hill over Haifa. Instead, Tel Aviv's most important urban signage is the beach and, more specifically, its 14km of shoreline.

There are a few exceptions, however. The iconic Shalom Meir Tower (9 Ahad Ha'am Street) may not be much to look at, but at 142m it was the tallest building in the Middle East when it was built in 1965. There's also Israeli artist Yaacov Agam's circular 'Fire-Water Fountain', which has illuminated Dizengoff Square since 1986. Agam is also responsible for the multicoloured façade of the city's renowned Dan hotel (see p016) on the seafront.

More recently, a clutch of striking residential structures has appeared, including the three Tzameret Towers on Pinkas Street, two Yoo towers by Philippe Starck on Mordechai Namir Road, and a Richard Meier-designed high-rise on Rothschild Boulevard, which is accented by IM Pei's First International Bank of Israel just up the road. Preservationists are still hoping that Tel Aviv's Bauhaus architectural treasures will one day assume the landmark status they so richly deserve. For the moment, it's usually only individual buildings that come under the renovator's wand.
For full addresses, see Resources.

Dizengoff Center

Opened in 1977, this was Israel's first
shopping mall, although these days
the Dizengoff Center can't be described
as its most lustrous. Tel Aviv's smaller
but more upscale Opera Tower Mall
(T 510 7496) and Azrieli Center (see p064),
located in two dazzling towers with an
observatory on the 49th floor, can claim
the more interesting settings. But it's
still worth visiting the Dizengoff Center,
situated on the lower floors of a mega
office complex, to sample the pick
of local brands. The best include Castro
(check out its massive flagship store,
T 525 5665), Fox (T 629 0558) and
Renuar (T 621 2400). Local clothes
are of a high standard and are sold
for low prices, compared to most basic
American or European brands. The
Dizengoff Center's Friday food market
is not to be missed.
50 Dizengoff Street, T 621 2400

Jaffa Clock Tower

The year 1906 marked 25 years of rule by Turkish sultan Abdul Hamid II throughout much of the Middle East and the Levant. To commemorate the occasion, a clock tower was built in the centre of Yafo (Jaffa). This was before the establishment of the modern Jewish city of Tel Aviv, and the three-storey tower became an immediate and iconic landmark, which has survived long past the expulsion of the Turks in 1917 by the British General Allenby. Today, the tower looms large as the quarter's geographic centrepoint, and its plaza leads beyond the original ancient walls to the modern city and Mediterranean beyond. Look for the tower's colourful mosaic windows. Created by artist Arie Koren during its renovation in 1965, they depict Jaffa's thousands of years of history.
Clock Tower Plaza, Yefet

Ben-Gurion Airport, Terminal 3

Moshe Safdie is perhaps best known for Habitat, his 1967 Montreal housing complex, but the Haifa-born architect has also delivered a striking monument in his homeland. Opened at Ben-Gurion Airport in 2004, the glass-and-steel structure of Terminal 3, which has a floor area of 117,000 sq m, is said to have run to a cool $1bn and was built in tandem with architects Skidmore, Owings and Merrill.

The largest construction project ever completed in Israel at the time, the terminal building is defined by a central passenger hall emblazoned with an oversized, abstract Star of David.
Ben-Gurion Interchange,
www.iaa.gov.il

Tel Aviv Port
More than 70 years after the first European refugees landed here, the port's seafront promenade received a sleek makeover to emerge as an attractive culinary and nightlife haunt. Try Gilly's (T 605 7777) for a champagne brunch and Mul-Yam (T 546 9920) for the crab, truffle and morel 'cappuccino'. In summer, round off your night at a free jazz performance.
Namal Tel Aviv

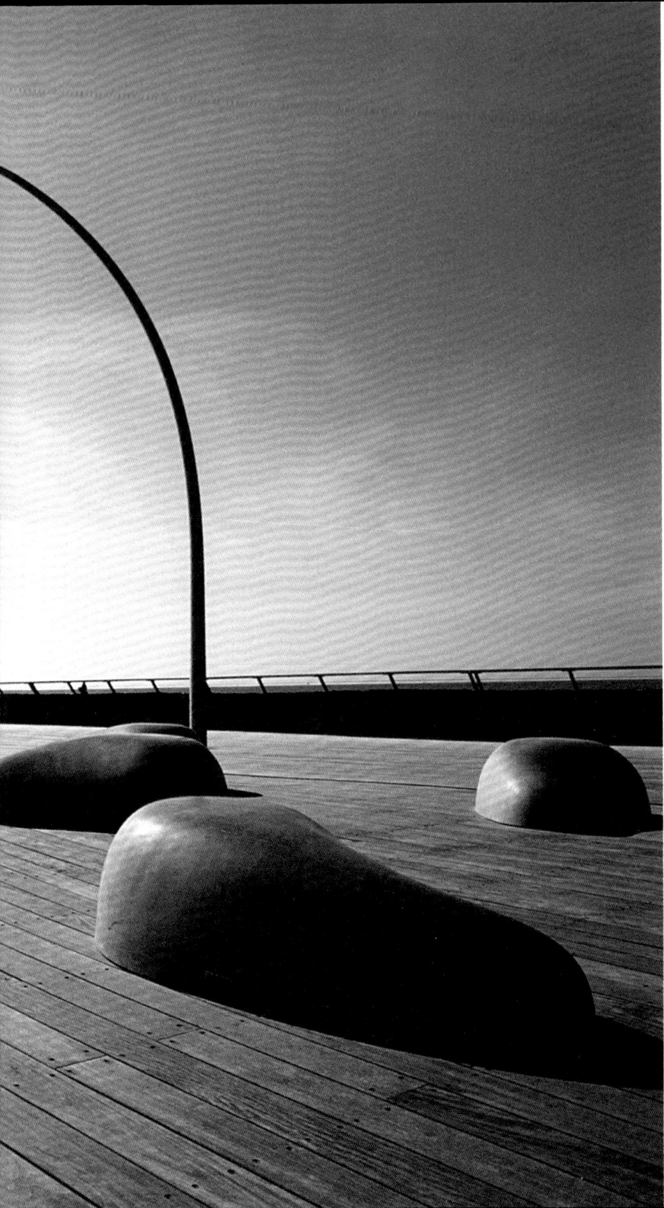

HOTELS

WHERE TO STAY AND WHICH ROOMS TO BOOK

Despite the presence of many of the major international brands, Tel Aviv (much like Israel itself) has never been known for its hotels. It's not that the city lacks decent lodgings, rather that it mostly has a shortfall in top-quality hotel staff. Blame it on Israel's socialist origins. A nation founded on kibbutz ideology with communal living and labour has been slow to get the hang of refined hospitality. That said, local hotels at the high, medium and low price level are improving their facilities and service, while a boom in design-driven boutique properties is raising the aesthetic standard. Arrivals such as Nina Cafe Suite (29 Shabazi Street, T 508 4141) and the Neve Tzedek Hotel (4 Degania Street, T 207 0706) are transforming southern Tel Aviv into the city's headquarters for the most stylish accommodation.

First-time visitors should opt for a location close to the beach for views of Tel Aviv's best asset: its Mediterranean shoreline. Most of the major hotels face the sea, with the swankiest, such as the Dan (99 Hayarkon Street, T 520 2552), offering Miami-style beach services. Despite the addition of designer offerings, such as Sea Executive Suites (76 Herbert Samuel Street, T 795 3434), the city has room for more. With international brands including Kempinski, Ritz-Carlton and W slated to open here in the coming years, it appears this gap in the market has been duly noted.
For full addresses and room rates, see Resources.

Gordon

Housed in a 1937 Bauhaus building in Tayelet, the Gordon is the result of a radical, meticulous renovation by Tel Aviv-based design collective 6B Studio. The original whitewashed modernist façade remains (above), while inside near-all-black public spaces and hallways lead to 12 clean-lined guest rooms. As well as Bauhaus-themed artwork and balconies, each offers something of a sea view; those facing the front are the best and the most atmospheric reservations. On the ground floor, there's a modern Mediterranean bistro, with both indoor and outdoor seating; upstairs, top up your tan in the convivial bar/lounge. Best of all is the service, which is refreshingly attentive and informative.
2 Gordon Street/136 Hayarkon Street, T 520 6100, www.gordontlv.com

Hotel Montefiore

A gem set in a restored 1920s building, the Montefiore has 12 chic rooms featuring Bauhaus furniture by Thonet and dark wooden floors, as in Room 16 (pictured). Owners Mati and Ruthie Broudo have lined the hallways with Israeli art. Israel's movers and shakers can be found in the bar and restaurant.
36 Montefiore Street, T 564 6100,
www.hotelmontefiore.co.il

Artplus Hotel

Tel Aviv may have been late in joining the art hotel craze, but the aptly named Artplus more than compensates for the delay. In the heart of Ben Yehuda – within easy walking distance of the beach, the Dizengoff Center (see p010) and White City – its location is ideal. Each of the five floors is devoted to an Israeli artist, among them Sigalit Landau and Zadok Ben David. The 62 rooms are compact yet comfortable, and are decorated with art (Room 201, opposite, shows the work of Elad Kopler), clean colours and modern furniture; the bathrooms are enclosed with glass. In the lobby (above), where free snacks are served every night, there's a small library of art books. Despite its contemporary vibe, the hotel offers a traditional Israeli breakfast buffet, replete with fruit, pastries and cheese.
*35 Ben Yehuda Street, T 797 1700,
www.atlas.co.il*

Brown
The debut property from Israeli group
Leopard Hospitality, the hip and friendly
Brown hotel inhabits an overhauled 1950s
bank, now done out in a myriad of, well,
brown tones. The once drab exterior has
been transformed into one of the city's
glossiest façades, while inside, Leopard
founder Leon Avigad, along with designers
Rubi Israeli and Ben Tauber, and architect
Dario Grunzweig, have carved out 30
rooms. These all continue the coffee-toned
theme and boast wooden floors, custom-
made furniture, canopied beds and
walk-in black marble showers; Deluxe
Room 110 (left) is one of the most
spacious options. The clubby reception
area is flanked by a bistro on one side and
a library on the other. The hyperrealistic
photography of Tel Aviv artist Pilpeled
appears throughout the hotel.
25 Kalisher Street, T 717 0200,
www.browntlv.com

24 HOURS

SEE THE BEST OF THE CITY IN JUST ONE DAY

In a city of only 88 sq km, you can see a lot in 24 hours. But this doesn't mean that everything is actually worth seeing. Lacking both historic landmarks and an immediately appreciable native architectural style, Tel Aviv requires focus and patience to conquer properly. Persevere and it'll be well worth the effort.

While the city's northern quarters have traditionally housed its élite, southern Tel Aviv is the focal point of the action. Roughly defined as the areas below Rothschild Boulevard, this is where Israel's early immigrant masses once huddled, where today Jews and Arabs attempt to coexist, and where the nation's often illegal foreign workforce is giving Israel some added spice.

In the past decade, Tel Aviv has become known as a city that never stops, and what it lacks in cultural interest it makes up for with its buzzing café scene and vibrant nightlife. That's not to say that the historic districts of Neveh Tzedek (see p028) and the biblical bastion of Old Jaffa should be neglected, it's just that the urban newcomers, such as Noga, Gan Hahashmal and White City, are Tel Aviv's current energetic heart.

Wherever you head, it's good to know that all that's unique about the world's only modern Jewish metropolis, with its equal parts glitz and grunge, is packed into our day, guaranteeing that you won't miss the best of what the city has to offer.

For full addresses, see Resources.

09.00 Manta Ray

With its prime location right on the Med, Manta Ray oozes atmosphere from the moment you set foot in the door, especially in the morning when the sun is not yet scorching. The restaurant is a popular dinner destination, but breakfast is the real treat here. As you laze just metres from the sea, pots of strong coffee are accompanied by numerous delicious local delicacies, from smooth tahini dip and spicy black olive paste to rich cheeses and freshly baked Balkan bread. If that isn't enough to power you up, eggs, omelettes, granola and Levantine salads are also on the menu. Arrive early, snag a terrace table and enjoy a languorous start to your day.
Alma Beach, T 517 4773

10.00 HaTachana

Tel Aviv's most unusual attraction is the redeveloped Jaffa train station, built in 1892 to link the ancient port with Jerusalem. Abandoned for more than 60 years, its elegant, Ottoman-era structures were renovated and reopened in 2010 as part of a 20 hectare complex of eateries, shops and a farmers' market. Admittedly, it can be touristy, but the development is charming and a success, partly thanks to its collection of local boutiques. Made in TLV (T 510 4333) designs quirky wares inspired by the city; Ronen Chen (T 516 0051) sells stylish womenswear; and the jewellery at Hella Ganor (T 576 6776) is eye-catching. There's plenty of alfresco dining and drinking; try the tapas at Shushka Shvili (T 516 0008) and coffee and sweet snacks at Café Greg (T 516 8887).
1 Koifman Street, www.hatachana.co.il

11.00 Neveh Tzedek

Today, the city's original Jewish quarter is a cultural, culinary and retail hub. This is the home of the Suzanne Dellal Arts Center (T 510 5656), renowned for contemporary dance, and the Chelouche Gallery (T 528 9713), which is located in the west wing of the historic Twin Houses. Designed by Russian-born, Bauhaus-era architect Joseph Berlin in the 1920s, the building is a rare example of local neoclassical architecture in a city where modernism is king. Shops to seek out in Neveh Tzedek include Mizo (T 516 4105), which sells Inbal Ben Zakeri's Japanese-influenced creations. On the edge of the area, heading towards White City, the white-cube Alon Segev Gallery (opposite, T 609 0769) represents Israeli contemporary artists, including Nir Hod, Arik Levy, Maya Zack and Guy Yanai.

12.30 Rothschild 12

As its name suggests, this eaterie/music venue is on Rothschild Boulevard, where Ottoman-era Neveh Tzedek melds into the Bauhaus White City. At first glance, the façade looks forlorn, if not decrepit. The exterior retains its original state, whereas the interior has been updated by owner Mati Broudo, who is also behind Hotel Montefiore (see p018) and the respected restaurants Brasserie M&R (see p051) and Coffee Bar (T 688 9696). Here Broudo has transformed an eclectic building, creating a light-filled restaurant at the front and an art and performance space at the back (which is where you enter). An upstairs gallery shows video art. In the evening, there are regular free acoustic sets by up-and-coming musicians. *12 Rothschild Boulevard, T 510 6430, www.rothschild12.com*

14.00 Bauhaus Foundation Museum
This museum on Bialik Square, curated by Daniella Luxembourg, is housed in a 1920s building restored by Russian-born architect Shlomo Gepstein in 1934. It's only 121 sq m but packs a punch with pieces by Marcel Breuer, Walter Gropius, Otto Lindig and Mies van der Rohe. Open by appointment, this is the ideal launch pad into Tel Aviv's Bauhaus core.
21 Bialik Street, T 620 4664

15.30 Tel Aviv Museum of Art
Harvard University architecture professor
Preston Scott Cohen was still relatively
unknown when he was chosen, in 2003,
to develop the new Herta and Paul Amir
wing of the Tel Aviv Museum of Art.
Opened in 2011, the extension is a far cry
from the brutalist aesthetic of the original
building; instead it is an exercise in angular
gestures, referencing some of Tel Aviv's
architectural influences, particularly Erich
Mendelsohn and the Bauhaus. Cohen's
1,858 sq m design is a series of twisting
geometric boxes wedged into a compact,
triangular site, its dramatic façade
composed of cast-concrete panels which
enclose a 27m atrium. The new wing will
almost double the museum's exhibition
space and, for the first time, provide
galleries devoted to the entire history of
the Israeli contemporary art movement.
*27 Shaul Hamelech Boulevard, T 696 1297,
www.tamuseum.com*

20.00 Social Club

Tucked down a blink-and-you'll-miss-it
alley off buzzy Rothschild, Social Club
is an all-hours bar and dining venue
serving a menu of bistro-style greatest
hits, from foie gras to *moules frites* and
hamburgers. Co-owner Yuval Barashi
previously worked in New York, and his
appreciation of that city's high-octane
food vibe is evident here. In the centre
is a U-shaped bar that attracts Tel Aviv's
bright young things. Fanning out from this
are dining areas spread over two floors,
including a striking black-and-white
striped space on the upper level. Social
Club is one of many ambitious bar/
restaurants to open in Tel Aviv in recent
years. Thanks to its creative cocktails,
well-executed cuisine and inviting
ambience, it's certainly one of the best.
*45 Rothschild Boulevard, T 560 1114,
www.socialclub.co.il*

23.00 Martha Kitchen + Bar

Set in the iconic Bauhaus-era ZOA building, owned by Israeli fashion designer Elie Tahari, this local hotspot is a short stroll from the Tel Aviv Performing Arts Center (see p060). An arty, cultured crowd arrives after hours for Martha's excellent wine list and vodkas infused with lavender, ginger and cinnamon.

26 Ibn Gabirol Street, T 696 6843

URBAN LIFE

CAFÉS, RESTAURANTS, BARS AND NIGHTCLUBS

High-end food culture in Israel is still evolving, but Tel Aviv's culinary scene has come a long way since the days when hummus and falafel were among the only options. Today, the quality of ingredients and the artfulness of presentation are impressive, and the cuisine's variety reflects a rich legacy of Turkish, Greek and Arab influences. Add more than two million recent immigrants from Asia, Africa and the former Soviet Union, and you'll come across dishes such as *khinkali* (traditional Georgian dumplings), which are on the menu at supper club Nanouchka (28 Lilienblum, T 516 2254). You'll also find top-notch tapas served at Vicky Cristina (1 Koifman Street, T 736 7272) and French-style meat dishes at Charcuterie (3 Rabbi Hanina, T 682 8843). For less formal dining, head to cafés such as Shine (38 Shlomo Hamelech Street, T 527 6186) and Comme Il Faut (Hangar 26, Tel Aviv Port, T 717 1550). Pick up juices and coffee at the kiosks on Rothschild and Ben Gurion, and fresh produce and homemade bread at the Farmers' Market (www.farmersmarket.co.il) at Tel Aviv Port.

One of the city's high points is its club culture – a mix of beachside dance parties in summer and European-style clubs in the cooler months. In addition, more intimate venues now lure night owls. The most design-driven, such as Evita (31 Yavne Street, T 566 9559), are at the core of Tel Aviv's gay scene. *For full addresses, see Resources.*

Herbert Samuel

Founder of Israel's first food movement, Jonathan Roshfeld opened this upmarket Levantine eaterie in 2007. The restaurant occupies the lower two floors of an office block and boasts a seafront location that has been capitalised on by its designers Alon Baranowitz and Irene Kronenberg. The architects installed floor-to-ceiling windows on the upper level to give coastal views and to flood the kitchen below with sunlight. On the ground floor, pergolas can be moved to create semi-private nooks. Waiters are happy to advise on the pan-Mediterranean wine list and menu, which includes a fine range of Italian charcuterie. We also recommend the pappardelle with chestnuts, and shredded short ribs. Open Thursday to Saturday. *Gibor House, 6 Koifman Street, T 516 6516, www.herbertsamuel.co.il*

Catit

Originally opened in 2002 in a remote farming village, Catit relocated four years later to a historic Ottoman-era villa, built as Tel Aviv's first hotel, in the Neveh Tzedek district. Architect Keren Shalom retained the structure's ornate shell, tile floors and elegant wall-stencilling, adding contemporary enhancements. The walnut bar is illuminated by organic, cell-shaped lamps. There are ground- and upper-level dining rooms, a garden to the rear and a streetside deck area – ideal for a cocktail event. The Levantine menu betrays the cordon bleu training of chef Meir Adoni.
4 Heichal Hatalmud Street, T 510 7001, www.catit.co.il

Shakuf

An Israeli artist-turned-chef, who has cooked everywhere from Per Se, Aquavit and WD-50 in New York to Copenhagen's Noma, Eldad Shem-Tov returned to his homeland to open Shakuf in a century-old Ottoman warehouse in Old Jaffa. Shakuf means 'transparent' in Hebrew – a quality reflected both in the restaurant's design and the Israeli menu. Forming the centrepiece of the 40-seat eaterie is a long, subtly illuminated, L-shaped bar (above), set around a glass-walled kitchen. Shem-Tov says that his dishes are intended to 'showcase the beauty of their raw materials'. The standouts for us include the sea trout cooked in cauliflower milk, and smoked quail's eggs, both served on oversized petri dishes.
2 Magen Avraham Street, T 758 6888, www.shakuf-rest.co.il

Hakosem

To declare a falafel joint Tel Aviv's best would be audacious, blasphemous even. Everyone here has their favourite place to order the piquant fried-chickpea snack, but Hakosem wins our vote for the flavour of its falafel, its atmosphere and ethnic inclusiveness. Spilling on to the street and located near the Dizengoff Center (see p010), Hakosem has a no-fuss interior, with a simple, cream-coloured décor.

Owner Mark Rosenthal says his falafel is 'new-wave-style' – coloured green or yellow, flecked with herbs and spices, and served in pitta with extras such as fried aubergine, salad, hummus, tahini and chips. Samples are almost forcefully offered by the smiley, multicultural staff.
1 Shlomo Hamelech Street, T 525 2033

Tzfon Abraxas

Eyal Shani is an epicurean Renaissance man, appearing on TV programmes, writing a celebrated newspaper column and helming a pair of Tel Aviv's top restaurants. His first was HaSalon (T 703 5888), a pricey, dinner-as-theatre 'supper club', whereas his second venue is a more modest affair. Situated in a former bar in Tel Aviv's social heart, Tzfon Abraxas is a split-level boîte that presents a modern take on Levantine classics.

On the ground floor is a bijou dining room with wooden tables and the original tiled floor. A curved staircase leads to the upper area and tiny open kitchen, from where Shani delivers his version of traditional regional dishes, such as grape-marinated lamb *schwarma* in a tahini sauce. The bar, which gets packed, is on the same level.
40 Lilienblum Street, T 678 6560

The Container

Swiss-born chef Vince Mustar made his
name with hit Tel Aviv restaurants such
as the Italian eaterie Vince and Tamar,
now called Cucina Tamar (T 639 0407),
and the meat-focused Charcuterie (T 682
8843). Now he has opened The Container,
an indoor/outdoor seafood restaurant
housed in a renovated waterfront hangar
in the Old Jaffa port. Oozing Levantine
charm, it's refreshingly informal, with
a 45-seat horseshoe-shaped bar defining
the space. Order one of the daily specials,
such as baby octopus with beetroot
salad, or seared tuna with a garlic confit,
accompanied by a beer or glass of wine.
The venue's cool vibe is enhanced by the
modern art on the walls and hipster DJs,
who play sets here several times a week.
Warehouse 2, Jaffa Port, T 683 6321,
www.container.org.il

Tapas Ahad Ha'am
This Spanish-themed eaterie is the
eagerly anticipated follow-up to chef
Jonathan Roshfeld's Herbert Samuel
(see p041). Located on the Bauhaus
Ahad Ha'am Street, the restaurant serves
a mean sangria and Iberian small plates.
Designed by Baranowitz Kronenberg,
the firm behind both Zepra (see p052)
and Herbert Samuel, Tapas Ahad Ha'am
is anchored around an open kitchen and
central wooden bar, which is lined with
an enticing array of Spanish products,
including jars of pickles, tins of salted
sardines and platters of sausage and
jamón. Despite the strong emphasis
on the food, from vegetable and meat
tapas-style dishes to hearty paellas,
the venue is also ideal for drinks. The
cava and sangria flow late into the night
watering a grown-up, sophisticated crowd.
27 Ahad Ha'am Street, T 566 6966

Dr Shakshuka

The dish *shakshuka*, a combination of tomatoes, garlic, eggs and spices cooked over a high heat, arrived in Israel from North Africa in the 1950s. Nowadays, it can be found all over the country, but the Dr Shakshuka version is considered the best in the city. Housed in a converted Ottoman warehouse and courtyard near Jaffa's labyrinthine fleamarket, this rustic restaurant serves up hundreds of orders of the tasty dish every day. Each is served in its own frying pan and comes with a hunk of white bread to wipe up any excess tomato chunks and juices – lest any of it should escape you. You could also try the couscous and *chraime*, a spicy Moroccan fish and vegetable stew. It's also worth watching friendly owner Bino Gabso manning the massive fiery stoves.
3 Beit Eshel Street, T 518 6560

Brasserie M&R

A taste of the Left Bank in the heart of Tel Aviv, Brasserie is complete with an art deco-tinged interior and authentic bistro menu. Open day and night, and boasting a prime city-centre location, it lures everyone from local politicians and celebrities to army officers and techie whizz kids. Do as they do and park yourself on one of the black-leather banquettes amid the brass fittings, high mirrors and cream-coloured walls. All the French classics are on offer, such as fresh oysters, steak tartare, pot-au-feu, boeuf bourguignon and coq au vin. If you like what you eat, pop into the next-door Brasserie Bakery, which sells sinfully rich pastries and great bread.
70 Ibn Gabirol Street, T 696 7111

Zepra
A project from acclaimed local chef
Avi Conforti and architects Baronowitz
Kronenberg, Zepra serves pan-Asian
cuisine inspired by traditional Asian
street markets. The large dining room
features an attractive parquet floor,
banquettes and dark wooden tables,
as well as an attention-grabbing lattice
lining the back wall and ceiling.
96 Yigal Alon Street, T 624 0044

INSIDER'S GUIDE

YAEL SPIEGEL, EDITOR

Journalist Yael Spiegel grew up in north Tel Aviv's placid suburbs. Now, though, she lives in the centre, near Dizengoff. 'I love the location because I'm so close to the beach,' she says. But the Mediterranean is not the only place Spiegel likes to play.

One of her shopping haunts is Aluma (9 Ashtori Harparchi Street, T 604 6095), a store brimming with covetable handmade and vintage clothes. For dinner, she might take a trip up the coast just north of Tel Aviv to Herzliya, where the whitewashed décor at Rocca (8 Ramat Yam Street, T 951 5122) provides the perfect backdrop for a relaxed meal. Other favourite pitstops include Toto (4 Berkowitz Street, T 693 5151), an Italian trattoria she favours for its elegant setting, and Cordovero (21 Cordovero Street, T 406 0771) in the hip Florentine district – a restaurant that has Spiegel 'drooling over its beetroot gnocchi'. Afterwards, she often goes to Taxidermy Bar (18 Harakevet Street), 'which is far enough from the beaten path to lure a hip, in-the-know crowd'.

For fun, it's off to laidback Hilton Beach in the city's north end. At weekends, the sands are packed with locals playing *matkot*, the 'national sport' of paddle tennis. Then Spiegel may zip down to HaTachana (see p026), which is 'filled with the best shopping and dining in town'. Another escape is Jerusalem (see p089), which has a 'magical atmosphere that is unrivalled in Israel', she says. *For full addresses, see Resources.*

ARCHITOUR
A GUIDE TO TEL AVIV'S ICONIC BUILDINGS

Thanks to its UNESCO World Heritage listing in 2003, this city has emerged as an island of cutting-edge charm in a sea of regional and global conflict. The designation celebrated Tel Aviv's historic quarter of White City (www.white-city.co.il), which boasts the world's richest concentration of surviving Bauhaus homes and offices. Indeed, so important is this area that it is only the second modern 'wonder' to receive the UNESCO award, following the futuristic Brazilian capital of Brasília.

Tel Aviv's Bauhaus heritage resulted from the intersections of European progressiveness and Middle Eastern practicality. From the 1920s, up to 5,000 buildings rose throughout the city in what are loosely described as the modernist, International or Bauhaus styles. Of this grouping, 750 are listed by UNESCO as municipal architectural treasures to be set aside for eventual restoration. Much as Istanbul's Ottoman heritage has been incorporated into its overall urban fabric, Tel Aviv has evolved around its Bauhaus legacy. The result is a city of unexpected design details, often hidden within offices, hotels, restaurants and bars. As for its contemporary face, Israel's buoyant economy means local developers have been able to attract architects such as Ron Arad (opposite), Massimiliano Fuksas (see p066), Richard Meier and IM Pei, who are all now leaving their mark on the city.
For full addresses, see Resources.

Design Museum Holon

In the town of Holon, 20 minutes south of Tel Aviv, the Design Museum is the area's first truly world-class arts institution and one of the most striking pieces of contemporary architecture in the country. The first major local commission for Anglo-Israeli architect Ron Arad, this $17m venue shows the work of both local and international designers in a split-level space set behind the swooping red steel façade (overleaf). The impressive shop features products curated by Tollman's, one of Israel's best design retailers. Located in a residential district, Arad's museum is the highlight of a nascent cultural quarter, which includes the Israeli Museum of Caricature and Comics (T 652 1849), and Mediatheque (T 502 1555). *8 Pinhas Eilon Street, Holon, T 215 1515, www.dmh.org.il*

Design Museum Holon

Tel Aviv Performing Arts Center
Completed in 1994, the $50m Performing
Arts Center was a collaboration between
Israeli architect Yacov Rechter and Ron
Arad, who was responsible for creating
the foyer and the lobby. Clearly, the
two did not work in unison. The Arad-
designed areas – gold-painted steps to
nowhere and oversized, abstract lighting
'cavities' – speak little of the modernist
arches that Rechter, in partnership with
his son Amnon, pasted on to the building's
exterior. Despite its aesthetic tension,
the building forms an impressive anchor
to this cultural compound east of the
city centre, which includes the Cameri
Theater (T 606 0960) and the Tel Aviv
Museum of Art (see p034).
19 Shaul Hamelech Boulevard, T 692 7777,
www.israel-opera.co.il

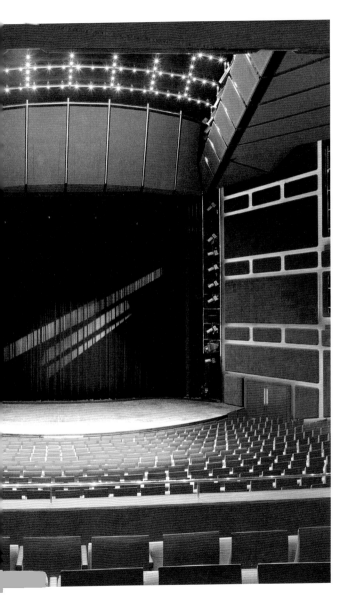

Yitzhak Rabin Center

Located on the site of an abandoned power station, near the university campus in Ramat Aviv, in the north of the city, the Yitzhak Rabin Center celebrates the life of the Israeli prime minister assassinated in 1995. The building was designed by the Israeli-Canadian architect Moshe Safdie and honours Rabin's legacy with a library, a museum and a research centre. The hilltop building retains the power station's original walls as its base and is capped by a pair of dramatic shell-like roofs crafted in Delft, Holland. The outdoor promenade looks out to Hayarkon Park and the Mediterranean beyond. Nearby are the Eretz Israel Museum (T 641 5244) and the Museum of the Jewish People (T 745 7800).
*77 Rokach Boulevard, T 745 3333,
www.rabincenter.org.il*

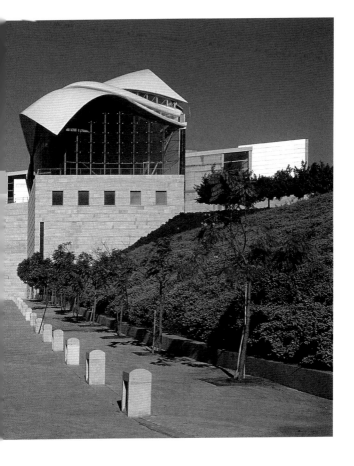

Azrieli Center

The Azrieli Center is to Tel Aviv what Canary Wharf is to London: a clutch of massive commercial structures on the fringes of what was once considered the city's real estate badlands. Set on a former parking lot for rubbish trucks, the three towers are designed in the shape of a circle, a triangle and a square. Inside, there are offices, gyms, shopping malls, cinemas and restaurants, as well as a top-floor observation deck that gives sweeping city views. The complex was named after David Azrieli, a Canadian developer and architect credited with introducing the shopping mall concept to Israel. Two of the towers were completed in 2000, with the square one, which currently houses a Crowne Plaza hotel, following in 2007.

132 Menahem Begin Road, T 608 1199

Cymbalista Synagogue

Completed in 1998, the Cymbalista Synagogue at Tel Aviv University was designed by Swiss architect Mario Botta, and is defined by a pair of circular towers around 12m high. In contrast to Tel Aviv's many austere cement-on-concrete constructions, the synagogue was built using a reddish stone from the Dolomite mountains for the exterior and a golden Tuscan stone within. Although modern in design, the structure alludes to biblical references, such as the columns at the entrance evoking the temple of King Solomon. Natural light flows in from above (there are no windows) and a lack of formal decoration emphasises the function of the main space as a place for prayer and meditation.
Tel Aviv University, T 640 8020,
www.tau.ac.il/institutes/cymbalista

Peres Center for Peace

The 200-year-old Arab neighbourhood of Ajami is filled with arched, Ottoman-style architecture and traditional Arab eateries. It is now also home to the 2008 Peres Center for Peace. Ten years in the making, this striking building, designed by Italian architect Massimiliano Fuksas, in collaboration with local firm Yoav Messer, is modest in size and slim in stature. The most impressive element is the façade, which is composed of alternating layers of concrete and glass. Rising seven floors, the centre is dedicated to promoting cross-cultural coexistence and includes a 200-seat auditorium, a library, a cafeteria, press hall and 10 apartments for visiting VIPs. The Mediterranean-facing gardens are open to the public.
132 Kedem Street, T 568 0680,
www.peres-center.org

Weizmann House

Perhaps best known for his iconic department stores, German architect Erich Mendelsohn spent a brief period in pre-Independence Israel, leaving a series of buildings that form much of the canon of influential early Israeli architecture. Although many are grander in scale, the 25-room Weizmann House, home of Israel's first president, Dr Chaim Weizmann, is Mendelsohn's most significant contribution to the nation's architectural treasury. Completed in 1937, it's one of the purest examples of the architect's style. A 1999 renovation by Hillel Schocken included the retouching of windows and glass panels, installation of air conditioning and the replastering of the façade.

Herzl, Rehovot, T 934 2111,
www.weizmann.ac.il

Kikar Habima
Perched on a hill overlooking the city, this
is one of Israel's most important cultural
realms. Built almost entirely from concrete,
in a modernist design, it comprises
Habima (the National Theatre); the Mann
Auditorium (the main concert hall for the
Israel Philharmonic Orchestra); the Helena
Rubinstein Pavilion for Contemporary Art
(part of the Tel Aviv Museum of Art); and
a garden. The complex was built between
1937 and 1957 and conceived mostly by
Zeev Rechter, who many consider to be
the doyen of Israeli architecture. Although
it's set on a busy intersection, it was once
mostly empty on nights when there were
no performances. The opening of bars and
restaurants on nearby Marmorek Street
has helped to lure a younger crowd. Plans
for its expansion are prompting vocal
debates among Israel's cultural vanguard.
2 Tarsat Boulevard, T 629 5555,
www.habima.co.il

SHOPPING

THE BEST RETAIL THERAPY AND WHAT TO BUY

Sadly, much of Israel's retail culture has retreated indoors. Blame it on the local climate, perhaps. With so many months of stiflingly hot and humid weather, air-conditioned malls have become the refuge of choice for shoppers in need of some meteorological respite. Tel Aviv's most important mall remains the Dizengoff Center (see p010), where Castro, Fox, Renuar and Golf – Israel's major homegrown brands – have flagship outlets.

Dizengoff Street is the city's main shopping thoroughfare, boasting smaller boutiques, including the hip Torso (110 Dizengoff Street, T 529 8339), whose limited-edition T-shirts make ideal gifts for boys back home. Similar stores can be found along Sheinkin Street, another haunt of Tel Aviv's trendier shoppers. Among these, Naama Bezalel (40 Sheinkin Street, T 517 5546) is worth a visit for its stylish skirts and dresses. For menswear, make a beeline for Sketch (see p076), while foodies should check out Olia (see p078), purveyor of the best local olive oils.

If your time is limited, head south to Old Jaffa and explore its ancient (or at least ancient-feeling) Fleamarket (Yefet Street), a great place to pick up bargain clothes, furniture and lots more. The best time to visit is on a Friday morning, when additional vendors set up stall. Stop for a falafel and a lemonade at an on-site eatery and enjoy Tel Aviv shopping at its Levantine best.
For full addresses, see Resources.

Aqua Creations

Up on the city's northern fringe, the well-established Israeli design brand Aqua Creations has finally opened a flagship store in Tel Aviv, showcasing the work of Israeli lighting and glass designer Ayala Serfaty. Her organic lamps appear in department stores and high-end hotels across the globe, from Bergdorf Goodman in New York to Milan's Nhow hotel. Serfaty's work is also displayed in the permanent collection at New York's MoMA. The designs on sale at Aqua Creations are ready to take home, but custom-made pieces can also be ordered from her sprawling, industrial atelier in the city's southern Noga quarter.
29 Ben Zvi Road, T 515 1222,
www.aquagallery.com

Elemento
Elemento began as a small-scale design shop on Rothschild Boulevard, before setting up a new home in Old Jaffa. Now housed in a renovated Ottoman-era building, it sells the collected works of Yossi Goldberg, who creates retro-edged furniture, from sofas to shelves, as well as artwork.
15 Hatzorfim Street, T 620 9848, www.elemento-design.com

Sketch

Tel Aviv's warm climate may make for an idyllic outdoor lifestyle, but its effect on local fashion is not so sublime, especially when it comes to men's clothes. This is why Sketch is such a revelation – and a revolution. Founder and chief designer Yossi Katzav made his mark while working for Israeli fast-fashion brand Castro, before decamping to New York in 2003 to lead the menswear team at DKNY. Back in Israel in 2009, he launched Sketch – his own men's label with a head-to-toe range including trousers and shirts, jackets and outerwear, as well as occasional suits. This is the complete package, with a slick brand identity, seasonal collections and a pair of sophisticated boutiques located in the north and the south (above) of the city.
2 Koifman Street, T 736 2640, www.ysketch.com

Shine

Since the mid-noughties, Shine has been a true local fashion pioneer, with a city-centre café (T 527 6186) that has become a Tel Aviv institution. There are two boutiques, on Masaryk Square (T 529 8609) and in Gan Hahashmal, which stock owner Alice Dahan's combat-chic-inspired pieces. The latter (above) is the brand's flagship store – a pared-down space selling the designer's most popular pieces, such as jeans, body-hugging tanks and simple A-line dresses, along with items from European designers including Freitag and Ilaria Nistri. Shine helped to kickstart Gan Hahashmal's fashion scene almost a decade ago, as the area was transformed into a hive of creativity. The brand's beach-ready, café-cool look has come to define Tel Aviv's style.

12 Harakevet Street, T 560 1658

Olia

As with grapes into wine, Israeli olives have been pressed into oil since biblical times. But the ancients were nowhere near as stylish as Olia, Israel's first haute olive-oil boutique. Designed by local architects Rose & Bloom and located a short stroll from the city hall, Olia's wood and glass boutique stocks numerous premium olive-oil blends, all certified extra virgin by the Israel Olive Authority and sourced throughout Israel and, depending on the harvest, the West Bank. Along with oils, Olia makes flavourful olive tapenades infused with Parmesan cheese or *za'atar* (Israeli oregano), as well as a collection of bath and body products. Ranging from shampoo to face scrubs, these items are made using organic, locally harvested olive oil, and produced exclusively in Mitzpe Ramon (see p102). *73 Frishman Street, T 522 3235, www.olia.co.il*

SPORTS AND SPAS

WORK OUT, CHILL OUT OR JUST WATCH

Owing to its sun, healthy cuisine and mandatory military service, Israel has always been a 'fit' nation. But it was only relatively recently that it developed a fitness culture. Today, health clubs, yoga centres, Pilates studios and bike clubs spring up seemingly every week. The best of these offer day passes; try the high-tech, centrally located Pure (77 Ben Yehuda Street, T 527 2782) or the upscale Cybex at the Hilton hotel (Independence Park, T 520 2222). Tel Aviv's gyms are generally smaller versions of their Western counterparts with, as befits a nation of a million Jewish mothers, elaborate on-site restaurants. Attitude is refreshingly low-key and members are usually eager to welcome visitors.

Unfortunately, the city's day spas have yet to meet the high standards found in Europe and the US in anything but price, and are, for the most part, not worth visiting. Two exceptions are Vila Spa (10 Yehuda Hamaccabi Street, T 546 0608) and Coola (Hangar 26, Tel Aviv Port, T 544 4462), which serves a female-only clientele. Along with yoga classes, it offers numerous types of massage and body treatments. City-sponsored fitness options have improved over the past few years. Many more cycle lanes have been introduced, including a path along the entire seafront, and a bike-sharing scheme is due to launch in 2011. In addition, the historic Gordon Pool (see p082) has been renovated.

For full addresses, see Resources.

Chandra Yoga Studio

Thanks to its location in the upmarket area of Bazel, close to the city centre and Dizengoff Street, and its American expat founder, Chandra is one of Tel Aviv's more stylish yoga studios. Launched in 2004 by New Yorker Lauren Ohayon, it offers classes mostly in Hebrew, though Ohayon does lead one or two sessions every week in English; the programme includes prenatal yoga, as well as classes for children, aged from four to seven. The studio's practice is based on the Vinyasa style, so expect the *asanas* (postures) to focus on movement and breathing.
4 Ashtori Hafarchi Street, T 546 4045, www.chandra-yoga.com

Gordon Pool

Perhaps because of its seafront setting, Tel Aviv lacks a decent array of public swimming pools. There is one exception, however. Opened in 1954, the Gordon has drawn locals of all ages for more than half a century. Comprising three seawater pools – one centrepiece Olympic-sized pool and two smaller ones for children and toddlers – it caters to all levels of swimmer. Up until a major renovation, which was completed in 2008, the site had a functional, boxy, uninspiring design, but now it connects more fluidly with the surrounding promenade and the beach, and boasts stylish wooden decking and palm trees. Serious lap swimmers arrive early in the morning, while a younger crowd, hopping between here and the beach, tends to dominate at the weekend. The pool is open from June to August only.

Tel Aviv Promenade, T 527 1555

Daniel Rowing Centre
Perched at the mouth of the River
Hayarkon and designed by Israeli firm
Plesner Architects, the Daniel Rowing
Centre offers a wide range of water
sports, such as canoeing and kayaking,
and a fitness centre. It serves those
from the city's northern districts, as
well as Israel's rowing élite. Call ahead
to book any of the facilities.
Rokach, T 699 0484, www.drc.org.il

Tayelet

The Tayelet (Hebrew for promenade) is Tel Aviv's Mediterranean front door, a strip of sandy coastline linking the city to the azure sea. Locals flock here, especially in the afternoons and into evening to witness glorious sunsets. Fitness is also a big part of beach culture and there are numerous sporting activities to get you in shape. Surfing is particularly popular and takes place from the city-centre shoreline to beyond Herzliya. Topsea Surfing School (T 432 9001) provides lessons and can kit you out with gear. The lack of hills and new cycle paths make this part of town ideal for a bike ride. Hire some wheels at O-Fun (T 544 2292), start at the promenade's north end and head south to Old Jaffa, which is around 40 minutes away.

ESCAPES

WHERE TO GO IF YOU WANT TO LEAVE TOWN

In a nation barely the size of the state of New Jersey, the idea of a proper escape usually involves leaving the country. But Israel has a vibrant leisure culture spread among rural, urban and seaside destinations. The most popular getaway is the Red Sea resort Eilat, an hour's flight south of Tel Aviv. Squeezed between Jordan and Egypt, it's an easy-going version of South Florida and a good base from which to explore Petra in Jordan. High-end weekenders have made Israel's northern Galilee region, now full of small inns, kibbutz guesthouses and spa resorts, another escape. Our favourite property here is the elegant Mizpe Hayamim (Rosh Pina, T 04 699 4555), an organic farm/spa resort set on a hillside with a pool and gardens, where they grow most of the food and the herbs used in the kitchen and the spa treatments. The snow-capped Mount Hermon is visible in the distance.

And you should travel to Jerusalem, which may be only an hour east of Tel Aviv but seems a world away from its commercialism and chaos. The best places to drop off your bags are the Mamilla Hotel (opposite) or the American Colony Hotel (23 Nablus, T 02 627 9777). Both give easy access to the markets of the Old City. Even if you are staying elsewhere, the Colony's cellar bar alone makes a visit worthwhile. Also head to the first-class Israel Museum (see p092), which has undergone a major renovation. *For all addresses, see Resources.*

Mamilla Hotel, Jerusalem

Nothing better signifies Jerusalem's new-found love of modern design than the Mamilla, opened in 2009. Close to the Old City and Downtown, the 194-room hotel was designed by architect Moshe Safdie, who clad the exterior in Jerusalem's pale local stone. The interiors were created by Italian designer Piero Lissoni, who has furnished the public areas, such as the lobby (above), and guest rooms with pieces by Boffi, Cassina and Alessi. The spa is second to none in the city. Head to the rooftop brasserie for great views and don't miss out the bar, which has a superb wine list. Adjacent to the hotel is Alrov Mamilla Avenue, a boutique-lined walkway linking West Jerusalem's modern heart with the Old City's ancient Jaffa Gate.
11 King Solomon Street, T 02 548 2222, www.mamillahotel.com

Executive Room, Mamilla Hotel

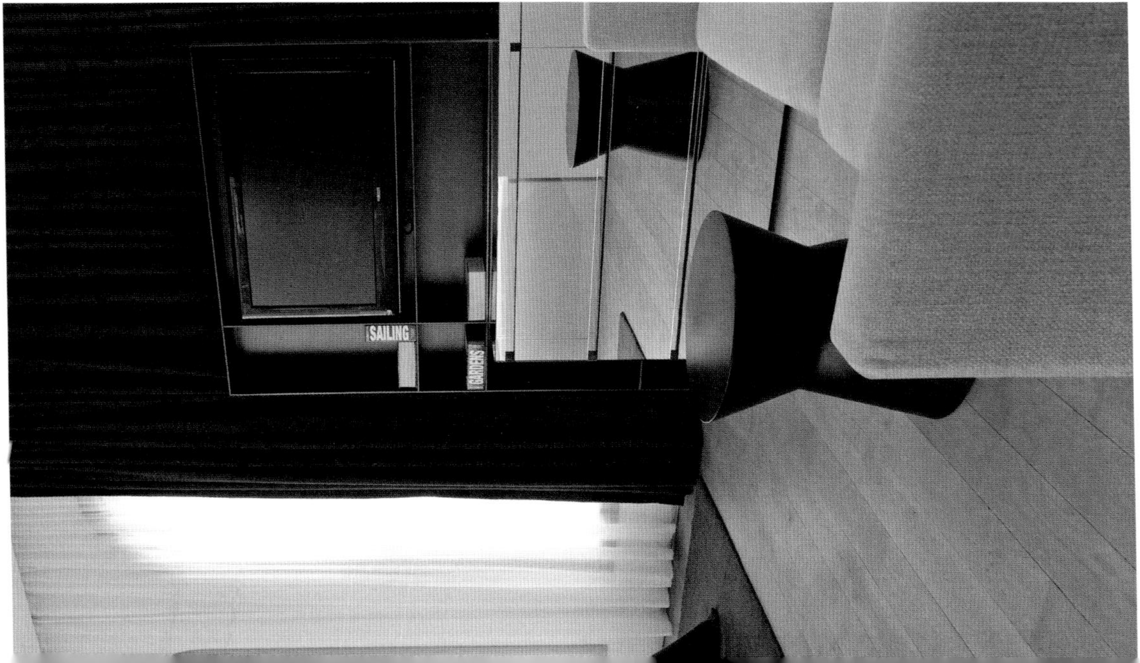
SAILING
GARDENS

Israel Museum, Jerusalem

Despite rising competition, this remains one of the most impressive arts venues in the Middle East. A $100m renovation and 2010 extension, designed by American architect James Carpenter, has boosted its appeal. Carpenter retained the museum's original 1965 modernist footprint, created by Alfred Mansfeld, adding terraces and glass pavilions (pictured). The result is an extra 18,500 sq m of gallery space and a more cohesive layout. Now there is room for site-specific works, by artists including Anish Kapoor and Olafur Eliasson, to sit alongside existing highlights such as Isamu Noguchi's sculpture garden and the Dead Sea Scrolls. Don't miss the Modern restaurant.

Ruppin Boulevard, T 02 670 8811, www.english.imjnet.org.il

Israel Museum

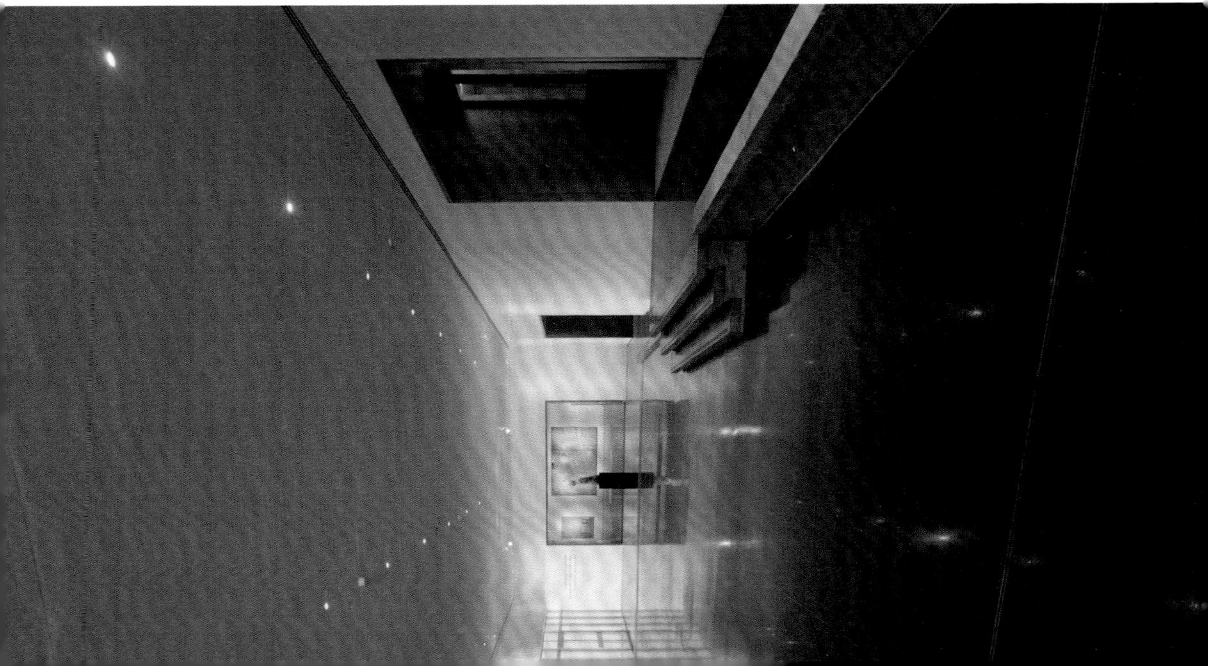

Yad Vashem, Jerusalem

After a decade of development and an investment of $100m, the History Museum at Jerusalem's Yad Vashem Holocaust memorial received a stunning makeover in 2005. The structure was designed by Moshe Safdie, who gave new life to this venerable 53-year-old institution overlooking the tranquil village of Ein Kerem. Spread over a massive 4,200 sq m (overleaf), Safdie's design stretches 180m in length and thrusts dramatically upward through the Mount of Remembrance, ending in a pair of curved 'wings'. Inside, the Hall of Names is an unsettling, 9m-high conical structure covered with the names of some three million Holocaust victims.
Har Hazikaron, Ein Kerem, T 02 644 3656, www.yadvashem.org

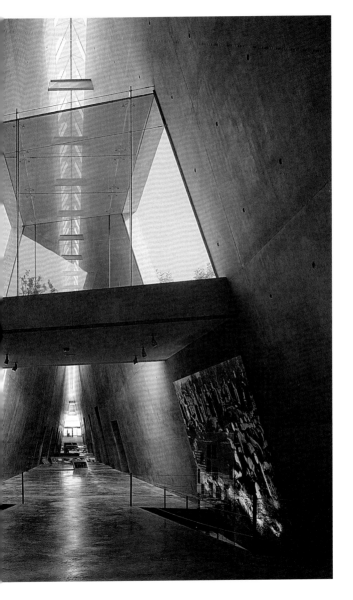

Yad Vashem, Jerusalem

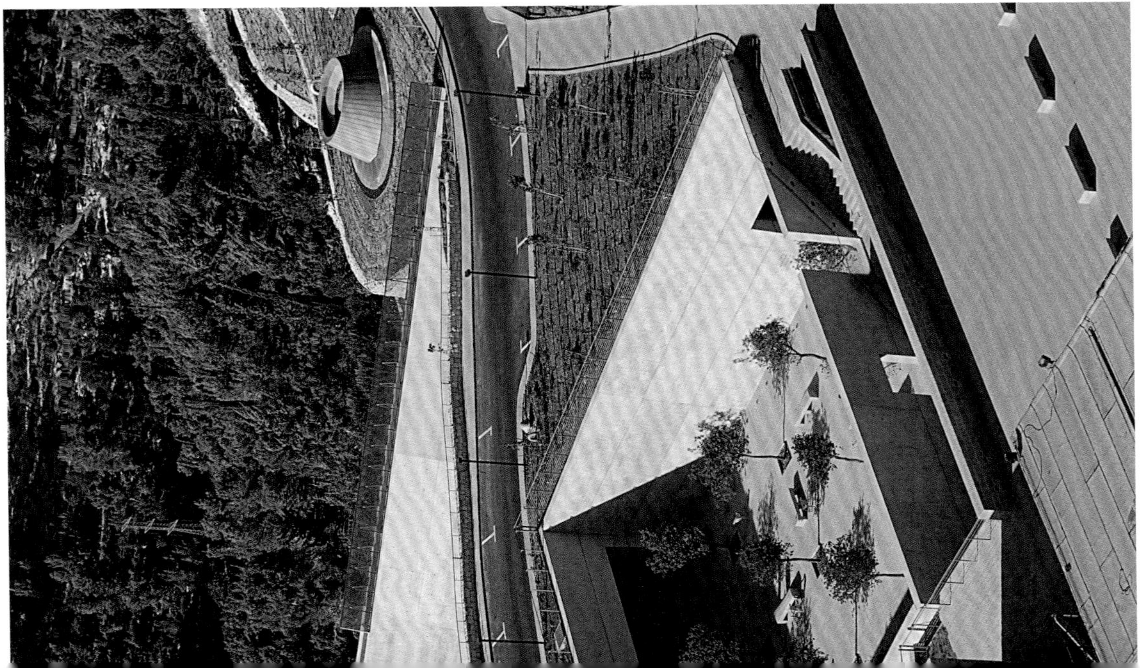

Dome of the Rock, Jerusalem
Built between 687 and 691 by Caliph
Abd al-Malik, the Dome of the Rock
is Jerusalem's best-known landmark,
a gold-capped mosque towering over
the Old City. Aesthetically, it dazzles
with its 20m-diameter gold-foil-covered
crown, but it remains a symbol of
contention, and has been the site of
intra-religious riots. Visits are usually
permitted in the early morning.

Chez Eugène, Mitzpe Ramon

Getaways in Israel tend to be in the wooded north rather than its arid south. One exception is Mitzpe Ramon, a town in the Negev that now boasts the chic Chez Eugène. Its six clean-lined rooms were designed by Frenchman Arnaud Rodrigue who fell in love with the area's stark landscape, while Tel Aviv chef Yair Feinberg runs the excellent restaurant. *www.mitzperamonhotel.co.il*

NOTES

SKETCHES AND MEMOS

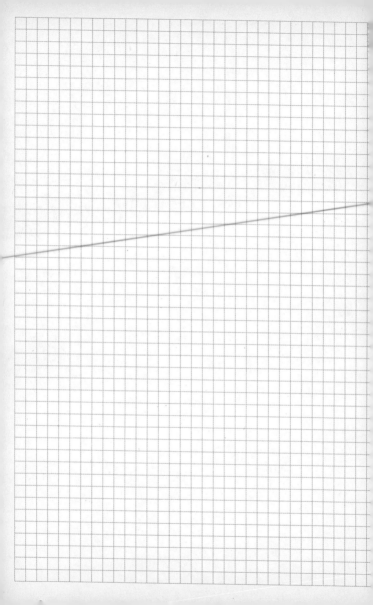

RESOURCES

CITY GUIDE DIRECTORY

A

Alon Segev Gallery 028
6 Rothschild Boulevard
T 609 0769
www.alonsegevgallery.com

Aluma 054
9 Ashtori Harparchi Street
T 604 6095

Aqua Creations 073
29 Ben Zvi Road
T 515 1222
www.aquagallery.com

Azrieli Center 064
132 Menahem Begin Road
T 608 1199
www.azrielicenter.co.il

B

Bauhaus Foundation Museum 032
21 Bialik Street
T 620 4664

Ben-Gurion Airport, Terminal 3 013
Ben-Gurion Interchange
www.iaa.gov.il

Brasserie M&R 051
70 Ibn Gabirol Street
T 696 7111

C

Café Greg 026
HaTachana
1 Koifman Street
T 516 8887

Cameri Theater 060
19 Shaul Hamelech Boulevard
T 606 0960
www.cameri.co.il

Castro 011
Dizengoff Center
50 Dizengoff Street
T 525 5665
www.castro.com

Catit 042
4 Heichal Hatalmud Street
T 510 7001
www.catit.co.il

Chandra Yoga Studio 081
4 Ashtori Hafarchi Street
T 546 4045
www.chandra-yoga.com

Charcuterie 040
3 Rabbi Hanina
T 682 8843

Chelouche Gallery 029
7 Mazeh Street
T 528 9713
www.chelouchegallery.com

Coffee Bar 030
13 Yad Harutzim Street
T 688 9696

Comme Il Faut Café 040
Hangar 26
Tel Aviv Harbour
T 717 1550
www.comme-il-faut.com

The Container 047
Warehouse 2
Jaffa Port
T 683 6321
www.container.org.il

Coola 080
Hangar 26
Tel Aviv Port
T 544 4462

HOTELS

ADDRESSES AND ROOM RATES

American Colony Hotel 088
Room rates:
double, from $380
23 Nablus Street
Jerusalem
T 02 627 9777
www.americancolony.com

Artplus Hotel 020
Room rates:
double, $195;
Room 201, $195
35 Ben Yehuda Street
T 797 1700
www.atlas.co.il/art-hotel-tel-aviv

Brown 022
Room rates:
double, $165;
Deluxe Room 110, $240
25 Kalisher Street
T 717 0200
www.browntlv.com

Chez Eugène 102
Room rates:
double, from $307
Har Ardon 8/1
Spice Quarter
Mitzpe Ramon
T 086 539 595
www.mitzperamonhotel.co.il

Dan 016
Room rates:
double room, from $370
99 Hayarkon Street
T 520 2552
www.danhotels.com

Gordon 017
Room rates:
double, $216
2 Gordon Street/136 Hayarkon Street
T 520 6100
www.gordontlv.com

Mamilla Hotel 089
Room rates:
double, from $390
11 King Solomon Street
Jerusalem
T 02 548 2222
www.mamillahotel.com

Hotel Spa Mizpe Hayamim 088
Room rates:
double, from $430
Rosh Pina
T 04 699 4555
www.mizpe-hayamim.com

Hotel Montefiore 018
Room rates:
double, $400;
Room 16, $400
36 Montefiore Street
T 564 6100
www.hotelmontefiore.co.il

Neve Tzedek Hotel 016
Room rates:
double, from $490
4 Degania Street
T 207 0706
www.nevetzedekhotel.com

Nina Café Suite 016
Room rates:
double, from $250
29 Shabazi Street
T 508 4141
www.ninacafehotel.com

Sea Executive Suites 016
Room rates:
double, $220
76 Herbert Samuel Street
T 795 3434
www.sea-hotel.co.il

WALLPAPER* CITY GUIDES

Editorial Director
Richard Cook

Art Director
Loran Stosskopf
Editor
Rachael Moloney
Author
David Kaufman
Deputy Editor
Jeremy Case
Managing Editor
Jessica Diamond

Designer
Lara Collins

Map Illustrator
Russell Bell

Photography Editor
Sophie Corben
Photography Assistant
Robin Key

Senior Sub-editor
Nick Mee
Sub-editor
Vanessa Harriss
Editorial Assistant
Ella Marshall

Interns
Francesca Burton
Aleeza Khan

**Wallpaper* Group
Editor-in-Chief**
Tony Chambers
Publishing Director
Gord Ray

Contributors
Jana Khoury
Daisy Ellen Omissi
David Saranga
Eytan Schwartz

Wallpaper* ® is a
registered trademark
of IPC Media Limited

First published 2007
Second edition (revised
and updated) 2011
Reprinted 2014

All prices are correct at
the time of going to press,
but are subject to change.

Printed in China

PHAIDON

Phaidon Press Limited
Regent's Wharf
All Saints Street
London N1 9PA

Phaidon Press Inc
180 Varick Street
New York, NY 10014

Phaidon® is a registered
trademark of Phaidon
Press Limited

www.phaidon.com

A CIP Catalogue record for
this book is available from
the British Library.

ISBN 978 0 7148 6658 1

PHOTOGRAPHERS

TEL AVIV
A COLOUR-CODED GUIDE TO THE HOT 'HOODS

OLD JAFFA
From the fleamarket haggling to the café culture, Israel's ancient rituals live on here

NOGA AND NEVEH TZEDEK
Art and media hub Noga rubs shoulders with the Ottoman-era charms of Neveh Tzedek

SHEINKIN
This chic strip attracts Tel Aviv's pretty young things, especially on the Sabbath

TAYELET
Watch the sun seekers and surfers at play on the city's famed promenade and beaches

GAN HAHASHMAL
Home to the local fashion scene and a host of organic eateries and bijou nightspots

DIZENGOFF
Packed with Israel's big-brand shops, this is where to go on a designer shopping spree

WHITE CITY
Come here to view the world's most outstanding examples of Bauhaus architecture

TEL AVIV PORT
Now a trendy haunt, whose sleek upgrade has lured both chic bars and lively markets

For a full description of each neighbourhood, see the Introduction.
Featured venues are colour-coded, according to the district in which they are located.